A Living Sacrifice

by
John MacArthur, Jr.

MOODY PRESS
CHICAGO

All Scripture quotations, unless noted otherwise, are from the *New Scofield Reference Bible,* King James Version. Copyright © 1967 by Oxford University Press, Inc. Reprinted by permission.

Library of Congress Cataloging in Publication Data

MacArthur, John, 1939-
    A living sacrifice / by John MacArthur, Jr.
       p.   cm.   — (John MacArthur's Bible studies)
    Includes indexes.
    ISBN 0-8024-5354-6
    1. Bible. N.T. Romans XII, 1-8—Criticism, interpretation, etc.
  2. Sacrifice—Biblical teaching. 3. God—Worship and love—Biblical
teaching. 4. Gifts, Spiritual—Biblical teaching. I. Title.
II. Series: MacArthur, John, 1939-   Bible studies.
BS2665.2.M213   1987
227'.106—dc19   87-25635
                                                          CIP

1 2 3 4 5 6 7 Printing/LC/Year 91 90 89 88 87

Contents

These Bible studies are taken from messages delivered by Pastor-Teacher John MacArthur, Jr., at Grace Community Church in Panorama City, California. The recorded messages themselves may be purchased as a series or individually. Please request the current price list by writing to:

WORD OF GRACE COMMUNICATIONS
P.O. Box 4000
Panorama City, CA 91412

Or call the following toll-free number:
1-800-55-GRACE

1

The Believer's Supreme Act of Spiritual Worship

Outline

Introduction
A. The Key to Spiritual Victory
   1. Sought
   2. Supplied
   3. Supported
B. The Epitome of Spiritual Worship
   1. Stated
   2. Symbolized
      a) 1 Samuel 15:22
      b) Psalm 51:17
      c) Psalm 141:2

Lesson
 I. Presenting Your Soul to God (v. 1a-c)
    A. The Pleading (v. 1a)
    B. The Prerequisite (v. 1b)
       1. 2 Corinthians 8:2-5
       2. Romans 8:8
       3. 1 Corinthians 13:3
       4. Matthew 13:20-21
       5. Matthew 19:16-22
    C. The Premise (v. 1c)
       1. The mercies identified
       2. The motive identified
II. Presenting Your Body to God (v. 1d-g)
    A. The Call to Make a Sacrifice (v. 1d)
       1. The importance of yielding your body
          a) Romans 6:12-13, 16, 19
          b) Romans 8:23

Introduction

The apostle Paul wrote the Christians in Rome, saying, "I beseech you therefore, brethren, by the mercies of God, that ye present your bodies a living sacrifice, holy, acceptable unto God, which is your reasonable service [spiritual worship]. And be not [continually] conformed to this world but be ye transformed by the renewing of your mind, that ye may approve what is that good, and acceptable, and perfect, will of God" (Rom. 12:1-2).

A. The Key to Spiritual Victory

 1. Sought

  A tearful, distraught young woman approached me when I was speaking at a conference and told me of her frustration—one I have heard of many times in my ministry. She said, "I just can't seem to live the Christian life the way I should. I am without victory or a sense of accomplishment because I struggle with the very simplest forms of obedience in my Christian walk. Can you help me? I have tried everything. I've been going to a church where they speak in tongues and have healings. I have spoken in tongues, prophesied, and been slain in the Spirit. Even though I've tried to get all I can get out of God, I am not pleased with my life." I replied, "That's your problem. The key to spiritual victory is not getting all you can get but giving all you have. There's a big difference."

2. Supplied

People today are seeking all sorts of spiritual experiences to receive more out of God. But the issue is not what they need to receive but what they need to give. That's the essence of Romans 12:1-8. Having concluded eleven chapters of profound and thrilling doctrine that defines what God has done for every believer, Paul does not say, "Here's what you need to receive." He says, "Now here's what you need to give." The key to powerful living is not that we receive more but that we give all we have.

3. Supported

In John 4:24 Jesus says the Father seeks true worshipers. In 1 Corinthians 6:20 Paul says God redeemed us that we might give Him glory. In fact, Paul identified Christians as those "who worship God in the spirit, and rejoice in Christ Jesus, and have no confidence in the flesh" (Phil. 3:3). Peter said, "Ye also, as living stones, are built up a spiritual house, an holy priesthood, to offer up spiritual sacrifices, acceptable to God by Jesus Christ" (1 Pet. 2:5). Christians are a kingdom of priests whose goal is to offer up spiritual sacrifices, even as priests of old offered up physical sacrifices before God.

B. The Epitome of Spiritual Worship

1. Stated

There are many kinds of spiritual sacrifices. Hebrews 13:15-16 says that our offering of praise and thanksgiving, as well as doing good works and sharing with others, are sacrifices pleasing to Him. But the supreme act of worship for a believer is to offer himself as a living sacrifice to God. Unfortunately that concept is quite distant from most of what is being purported today as keys to spiritual living. Scripture doesn't say that spiritual victory is a matter of affirming your self-worth or of seeking something more; it's a matter of presenting yourself as a living sacrifice.

The truth of Romans 12:1-2 is the sum of eleven chapters of doctrine. It is not an arbitrary thought pulled out of the air. Sacrificial worship is the natural response of the Christian who realizes all that God has done for him. The supreme act of spiritual worship is giving back to God all that we are. That may not be easy, but it is necessary if we are ever to know the fullness of God's blessing and be able to render to Him the service due to Him. However, many Christians flirt with the world and with their fleshly desires. They become victims of the world's philosophy and values, so they never make the total commitment discussed in those two verses. Consequently they forfeit the fullness of the blessing God would have for them.

2. Symbolized

In the Old Testament an Israelite would come to God bringing to the priest at the Tabernacle or Temple the animal he was going to sacrifice. The priest slew the animal and placed it on the altar as an offering to God. That system came to an end with the cross of Christ. God no longer desires that animals be offered to Him—but living men and women. Whereas the essential act of the Old Testament believer was presenting a sacrifice as an indication of the genuineness of his faith, the essential act of a New Covenant believer is presenting his heart, soul, and mind as a living sacrifice. That doesn't mean, however, that the Old Testament believer was exempt from being a living sacrifice. The animal was a symbol of his life. God has always wanted us to present Him with a lifetime of wholehearted service.

a) 1 Samuel 15:22—Samuel said, "Hath the Lord as great delight in burnt offerings and sacrifices, as in obeying the voice of the Lord? Behold, to obey is better than sacrifice." The answer to that rhetorical question is no. A dead animal was offered only as an outward symbol of the presentation of one's heart and soul.

b) Psalm 51:17—David said, "The sacrifices of God are a broken spirit; a broken and a contrite heart, O God, thou wilt not despise."

c) Psalm 141:2—David said, "Let my prayer be set forth before thee as incense; and the lifting up of my hands, as the evening sacrifice."

In the New Testament, God calls only for the living sacrifice—a call to the dedication of oneself to His will. It is the only logical response to His redeeming work.

What does it mean to offer ourselves as a living sacrifice? Romans 12:1-2 presents these four elements of a living sacrifice foundational to our spiritual experience: the offering of a believer's soul, body, mind, and will.

Lesson

I. PRESENTING YOUR SOUL TO GOD (v. 1*a-c*)

A. The Pleading (v. 1*a*)

"I beseech you."

The Greek word translated "beseech" (*parakaleō*) can mean "to come alongside" or "to exhort with tenderness." With the authority of an apostle and the tenderness of a brother in Christ, Paul entreats the believers in Rome to follow through with the natural response to salvation. He made a similar entreaty to Philemon: "Though I might be much bold in Christ to enjoin [command] thee that which is fitting, yet for love's sake I rather beseech thee" (Philem. 8-9).

11

B. The Prerequisite (v. 1*b*)

"Brethren."

Jesus said, "What is a man profited, if he shall gain the whole world, and lose his own soul?" (Matt. 16:26). Scripture refers to the soul or spirit as that inner part of man that God seeks to redeem. It is the invisible part—the essence of our being—that must be given to God. Paul's use of the Greek word translated "brethren" implies a call to a regenerated soul to make a proper offering. Only those who know the Lord can present themselves as living sacrifices.

The starting point of offering yourself to God begins with first offering your soul to Him. If your soul has not been born again, there's no way you can properly respond to God. Nothing else can be offered to God if the soul hasn't been offered. An unregenerate person cannot give God his body, mind, or will in service. In fact, he cannot respond to God at all. Unbelievers are spiritually dead (Eph. 2:1). First Corinthians 2:14 says the unsaved or natural man does not understand the things of God; they seem foolish to him. The appeal of Scripture and the Spirit to make a supreme act of dedication to God is to the believer.

1. 2 Corinthians 8:2-5—The churches of Macedonia were poor and were experiencing great trials. Nevertheless they joyfully and generously gave to provide for the needs of others, even beyond what they could afford. Verse 5 tells us what enabled them to give so sacrificially: "This they did . . . first [giving] themselves to the Lord." That was the key.

2. Romans 8:8—Paul said, "They that are in the flesh cannot please God." A person who is "in the flesh" is not saved. Such an individual cannot make an acceptable offering of anything to God, let alone his life. An unbeliever may believe he is serving God, but unless he has offered his soul to God by being saved, he cannot acceptably offer his body, mind, or will.

3. 1 Corinthians 13:3—Paul expressed that truth in these well-known words: "Though I bestow all my goods to feed the poor, and though I give my body to be burned,

and have not love, it profiteth me nothing." So if I don't possess the love of God, all my acts of self-sacrifice and charitable contributions to the poor are worthless. They don't mean a thing to God. Only when our innermost self has experienced the saving mercy of God do we have the power and motivation to live a life of sacrifice to God.

4. Matthew 13:20-21—In the parable of the sower, Jesus taught that people's hearts are like different kinds of soil. In the rocky soil the roots of the seedlings couldn't penetrate deep enough to find water and nutrients, so the sun caused them to wither and die. The Lord compared the rocky soil to one who hears the gospel and has a favorable response to it, yet falls short of actually believing. When such people encounter trials or persecution, they lack the roots of faith, which are necessary for assimilating spiritual nourishment. Such people may immediately respond in joy to the truth about Christ, but their lack of faith when circumstances call for a sacrifice means that they never really had genuine saving faith. The soul never truly given to God cannot make any other sacrifice.

5. Matthew 19:16-22—When Jesus told the rich young ruler to sell what he had and give to the poor to acquire eternal life, "he went away sorrowful" (v. 22). He was not willing to make such a sacrifice in obeying the Lord.

C. The Premise (v. 1c)

"By the mercies of God."

1. The mercies identified

Believers have experienced the mercies of God. That is the basis for Paul's entreaty to dedicate our lives to God. The mercies of God refer in general to everything God has done for the believer. Note what Paul has mentioned so far in Romans 1-11:

a) Love (5:5; 8:39)

b) Grace (4:4; 5:2)

c) The Holy Spirit (5:5; 8:2-26)

d) Peace (1:7; 2:10)

e) Faith (10:17)

f) Comfort (8:14-18, 28, 35-39)

g) Power (1:16)

h) Hope (5:2; 8:24)

i) Patience (5:3; 11:22)

j) Kindness (2:4)

k) Glory and honor (2:10; 9:21-23)

l) Righteousness (3:21-22; 5:17-18)

m) Forgiveness (3:25; 4:7-8)

n) Reconciliation and justification (5:9-10)

o) Security (8:26-39)

p) Eternal life (5:21; 6:22-23)

q) Freedom (6:18; 7:5-6)

r) Resurrection (8:11, 23)

s) Sonship (8:14-17)

t) Intercession (8:27)

2. The motive identified

What should be our response since we have received so much yet deserve so little? Our gratitude for those divine benefits ought to be the strongest motivation to live our lives for God. Paul could have threatened us with judgment, but he didn't. Gratefully giving our lives to God in service is the logical response of those who have received the infinite mercies of such a gracious God. To hold back is an incredible act of ingratitude.

The psalmist demonstrated the proper response in Psalm 116:12: "What shall I render unto the Lord for all his benefits toward me?" There is nothing we could return that would be equal to what He has done for us. But fortunately He doesn't expect us to return in kind. All He asks is that we give ourselves as a living sacrifice. The greatest desire of a Christian is to give all that he is and has to Jesus Christ.

Doctrine Before Duty

Sometimes people tell me my sermons need to be less doctrinal and more practical. That may be true, but the apostle Paul is the one who set the pattern of giving doctrine before exhorting people to fulfill their duties. In Romans Paul doesn't give many exhortations until after he has given eleven chapters that focus primarily on doctrine.

Paul's emphasis on doctrine is evident in his exhortation for Timothy to be "nourished up in the words of faith and of good doctrine" (1 Tim. 4:6). He told Titus that an important principle of ministry is for an elder to be "holding fast the faithful word that . . . he may be able by sound doctrine both to exhort and confute the opposers" (Titus 1:9). We exhort others on the basis of truth.

Paul, reveling in the incomprehensible heights of doctrinal truth, exclaimed, "Oh, the depth of the riches both of the wisdom and knowledge of God! How unsearchable are his judgments, and his ways past finding out! For who hath known the mind of the Lord? Or who hath been his counselor? . . . For of him, and through him, and to him, are all things: to whom be glory forever. Amen" (Rom. 11:33-34, 36). Next he said, "Present your bodies a living sacrifice" (12:1). Similarly, in the epistle to the Galatians he gives four chapters of doctrine before giving two on duty. In Ephesians he gives three chapters on each, and in Colossians he gives two chapters on each. All behavior is predicated on doctrine. Ethics rise out of dogma.

That's what Jesus was communicating when He said, "If ye know these things, happy are ye if ye do them" (John 13:17). Before you can be happy in doing something, you have to understand it. Peter approaches the principle from the opposite perspective: forgetting what you know will stunt your Christian growth (2 Pet. 1:9). James warns us about becoming forgetful hearers by not applying the doctrine we have heard (James 1:22-25).

Duty is always based on doctrine. There has to be a foundation of truth before there can be any call to a certain kind of behavior. Although practical applications are important, an emphasis upon the practical at the expense of doctrine betrays a shallow perception of what motivates people to do things.

Presenting yourself as a living sacrifice begins with coming to Christ in faith and receiving Him as Savior and Lord. The salvation of your soul is the starting point of giving yourself to God.

II. PRESENTING YOUR BODY TO GOD (v. 1*d-g*)

A. The Call to Make a Sacrifice (v. 1*d*)

"Present your bodies."

The exhortation to present our bodies conveys the idea of surrendering or offering a sacrifice. God wants us to yield our bodies to His will. He already has the soul—the inner man—that which has already been transformed by His saving grace. However, yielding one's body to God isn't always easy, because the body is the beachhead of sin in the life of the redeemed. When a Christian dies, his spirit goes to heaven, and his body goes to the grave. Once that separation is made, there's no longer a struggle with sin—that which Romans 7:15-25 so clearly describes.

1. The importance of yielding your body

Paul stressed the importance of yielding the body to God many times.

a) Romans 6:12-13, 16, 19—Paul said, "Let not sin, therefore, reign in your mortal body. . . . Neither yield ye your members as instruments of unrighteousness unto sin, but yield yourselves unto God.

. . . Know ye not that to whom ye yield yourselves servants to obey, his servants ye are whom ye obey, whether of sin unto death, or of obedience unto righteousness? . . . Yield your members servants to righteousness, unto holiness." Although sin no longer reigns in the redeemed soul, it still manifests itself occasionally in our unredeemed flesh.

b) Romans 8:23—The corruptible, unredeemed body eagerly waits to experience the fullness of our salvation—glorification. Our souls have been redeemed, but our bodies have not yet been.

c) 1 Corinthians 6:19—Paul said, "Know ye not that your body is the temple of the Holy Spirit who is in you?" Our redeemed souls are encased in our humanness, in which sin finds its expression.

d) Romans 7:25—Paul recognized that it was not his redeemed soul causing him to sin but his sinful flesh. He identified the battle between his flesh and his new nature in these words: "With the mind I myself serve the law of God; but with the flesh, the law of sin."

e) 1 Thessalonians 4:4-5—Paul said, "Every one of you should know how to possess his vessel [body] in sanctification and honor, not in the lust of sensuality, even as the Gentiles who know not God."

f) Philippians 3:21—When Christ returns He "shall change our lowly body, that it may be fashioned like his glorious body." We long for our glorification, but until that time comes we must present the imperfect bodies we now have as living sacrifices to God.

2. The difficulty of yielding your body

It is scary to see the way the body can dominate the soul. Although we are redeemed creatures with souls that have been transformed and indwelt by the Spirit of God, it is remarkable how much the body can resist the work of the Spirit. The body is the center of desire, disease, depression, and doubt. However, it must continually be brought into subjection and offered to God as a living sacrifice.

Paul gives us insight into the difficulty of yielding our bodies to God. In 1 Corinthians 9:27 he says, "I keep under [control] my body, and bring it into subjection, lest that by any means, when I have preached to others, I myself should be a castaway [disqualified]." Paul knew that to represent Christ effectively, he had to control his physical appetites.

Gnostics and others in ancient Greek circles had a low view of the body, depreciating its value. They had a dualistic philosophy asserting that spirit is good but matter is evil. That kind of thinking has been reflected in Christian circles by those who say we shouldn't bother with church discipline (Matt. 18:15-17) because a person's unredeemed body can't be corrected anyway. But that's not what Scripture says. You can bring an unredeemed body under the subjection of the Holy Spirit. Whenever your body is used for divine purposes, it becomes an instrument of righteousness (Rom. 6:13). Whenever it is involved in something that displeases God, it is an instrument of unrighteousness. The Bible doesn't teach that dualistic view and conclude that the body is of no consequence. After all, our bodies will one day be redeemed. There is no place for any teaching that tolerates sin in the Body of Christ.

Vice was so rampant in biblical times—as it is in our day—that people tended to be tolerant of sin. Christians have no business reading books, listening to music, or watching TV shows and movies that are filled with adultery or other sins that may be acceptable to society. If we have become tolerant of those kinds of things, we need to remind ourselves of Paul's words in 1 Corinthians 6:12-13: "All things are lawful unto me, but all things are not expedient; all things are lawful for me but I will not be brought under the power of any. . . . The body is not for fornication, but for the Lord; and the Lord for the body." The Lord can't work through you unless He works through your body. And there can be no sanctification that does not include the body. In 1 Thessalonians 5:23 Paul says, "The very God of peace sanctify you wholly; and I pray God your whole spirit and soul and body be preserved blameless unto the coming of our Lord Jesus Christ." The same body through which our old nature expressed itself is to be the vehicle of our new nature.

B. The Character of the Sacrifice (v. 1e-f)

1. It must be living (v. 1e)

"A living sacrifice."

A living sacrifice is a definite contrast to the Old Testament sacrificial system, where the body of a dead animal was offered. What God now wants are living sacrifices.

a) Explained

The advantage of a living sacrifice is that it can be a perpetual offering, as compared to an animal sacrifice, which was slain and consumed. God desires something that does not die or become consumed.

The account of Abraham and Isaac in Genesis 22 is an illustration of a living sacrifice. Abraham was told by God that he would become the father of a great nation, whose children would be as numerous as the stars of the heavens. Because Sarah, his wife, was past her child-bearing years, it was only through God's marvelous intervention that Isaac, the son of promise, was born to them. To test Abraham's trust in Him, God said, "Take now thy son, thine only son Isaac, whom thou lovest, and get thee into the land of Moriah; and offer him there for a burnt offering" (v. 2). Although Isaac was Abraham's heir and the key to all of God's promise to him, Abraham obediently prepared to offer Isaac, whom God spared at the last moment. Although Isaac would have been a dead sacrifice, Abraham would have made a living one: he determined to serve God, even if that meant living the rest of his life without his beloved son.

God isn't asking us to die; He wants us to be willing to live the rest of our lives in complete obedience to Him. Abraham was willing, and that made him a great man. He was willing to offer himself to God no matter what the cost. A living sacrifice—a humble, obedient surrender of self to God—is the basis of true worship. It is the foundation of all Christian service. That is what Paul meant when he said he was "always bearing about in the body the dying of the Lord Jesus" (2 Cor. 4:10). He told the Philippians, "For to me to live is Christ, and to die is gain" (Phil. 1:21), and, "I have suffered the loss of all things, and do count them but refuse, that I may win Christ" (Phil. 3:8).

b) Exemplified

David Livingstone, the great nineteenth-century Scottish missionary to Africa, said, "People talk of the sacrifice I have made in spending so much of my life in Africa. Can that be called a sacrifice which is simply paid back as a small part of the great debt owing to our God, which we could never repay? Is that a sacrifice which brings its own reward of healthful activity, the consciousness of doing good, peace of mind, and a bright hope of a glorious destiny hereafter? Away with such a word, such a view, and such a thought! It is emphatically no sacrifice. Say rather it is a privilege. Anxiety, sickness, suffering or danger now and then, with a forgoing of the common conveniences and charities of this life, may make us pause and cause the spirit to waver and sink; but let this only be for a moment. All these are nothing when compared with the glory which shall hereafter be revealed in and for us. I never made a sacrifice. Of this we ought not to talk when we remember the great sacrifice which He made who left His Father's throne on high to give Himself for us" (cited in Paul Lee Tan's *Encyclopedia of 7,700 Illustrations* [Winona Lake, Ind.: BMH, 1979], p. 1178; and reflected in *Livingstone's Private Journal: 1851-1853*, ed. I. Schapera [London: Chatto & Windus, 1960], pp. 108, 132). Ironically, those who make a living sacrifice usually don't see it as such.

20

2. It must be holy (v. 1*f*)

"Holy, acceptable unto God."

An animal presented as a sacrifice in the Old Testament was required to be without blemish. It was to be the best of the flock or herd. The Greek word translated "holy" (*hagios*) means "set apart." It did not convey the idea of being pure and undefiled because the Greek gods were as sinful as the men who worshiped them. The New Testament in particular gave it the connotation of purity and freedom from sin. God wants your body—not to mention your mind, will, and emotions—to be brought into subjection to His will and offered to Him as a living sacrifice.

We have become so comfortable in our society. We're willing to serve the Lord if it doesn't cost us too much time or energy, or doesn't conflict with our favorite television program. We may desire to offer ourselves as a living sacrifice to God but hesitate to give Him everything. We often prefer to indulge in worldly pleasures and pursuits and the temporal sense of security and significance they offer. God does not want commitments that are half-hearted. Only those that are self-sacrificing and unblemished by wrong motives or insincerity will do.

What are you offering God? When you say, "I want to give my life to the Lord," what is it you're giving? Only pure and total devotion is acceptable to God. Anything else is not. The Lord indicted the Israelites for their half-hearted devotion, saying, "You are presenting defiled food upon my altar. . . . When you present the blind for sacrifice, is it not evil? And when you present the lame and sick, is it not evil? Why not offer it to your governor? Would he be pleased with you?" (Mal. 1:7-8, NASB*). Instead of bringing the best of their flocks, many of the Israelites were bringing the worst to be offered to God. They certainly wouldn't have offered such inferior payment to the governor for taxes but were content offering it to God. The Israelites' fear of God motivated them to offer a sacrifice, but it was an inferior sac-

New American Standard Bible.

rifice, which they would not have offered had they truly loved God. Do you do out of fear what you will not do out of love for God?

Only a holy sacrifice is acceptable to God. The Greek word translated "acceptable" means "well-pleasing" or "satisfactory." Hebrews 13:16 says, "To do good and to share forget not; for with such sacrifices God is well pleased." God is satisfied when we do good to others and help those in need.

C. The Consecration of the Sacrifice (v. 1g)

"Which is your reasonable service."

"Service" (Gk., *latreia*) can also be translated as "spiritual worship." It is used in the Septuagint (the Greek version of the Old Testament) to refer to worshiping God according to the Levitical law. It is used in Hebrews 9:6 to refer to the priestly service of presenting offerings and sacrifices. And here in Romans 12:1 it is used of the believer's act of offering up his body as a spiritual priest in consecrated sacrifice to God.

The worship is described as reasonable, a translation of the Greek word *logikos*, from which comes the English word *logic*. The worship God accepts involves the reasoning process of the inner man, rather than an automatic response void of a conscious choice. Whereas in the Old Testament dead sacrifices were offered as external acts, Paul is emphasizing a living sacrifice that is an act of internal worship. God wants spiritual worship—an intelligent, heartfelt, consecrated devotion—rather than just physical and mechanical religious activity. True worship does not consist of elaborate prayers, a certain liturgy or ritual, candles, robes, stained glass, classical religious music, or feeling spiritual goose bumps in a church service; it is the spiritual act of devoting your body to holy living for the glory of God. God isn't looking for you to offer some isolated act of worship or natural talent; He is looking for you to give yourself.

III. PRESENTING YOUR MIND TO GOD (v. 2a-b)

"Be not conformed to this world, but be ye transformed by the renewing of your mind."

One of the keys to being able to offer your body is to be sure that your mind has been renewed. It is the mind that chooses whether we will express our new nature through holy living or allow our flesh to act unrighteously.

A. A Negative Conformation (v. 2a)

"Be not conformed to this world" (Gk., *aiōn*).

Paul says that Christians are not to be conformed to this world (lit., "age"). That is a reference to any unbiblical philosophy of life. Archbishop Richard Chenevix Trench, a renowned Greek scholar of the nineteenth century, defined it as "that floating mass of thoughts, opinions, maxims, speculations, hopes, impulses, aims, [and] aspirations, at any time current in the world" (*Synonyms of the New Testament* [Grand Rapids: Eerdmans, 1973 printing], pp. 217-18). It is akin to the German concept of *zeitgeist*, the general intellectual, moral, and cultural climate of an era.

Satan, of course, is the prince and ruler of the world's system. It is the instrument through which he promotes his goals and ambitions, and it is characterized by pride and ungodly morality. We see evidence of it in professional sports, in music, and in movies and other forms of media. The apostle John states that "the whole world lies in the power of the evil one" (1 John 5:19, NASB).

The Spirit of God calls us to stop allowing ourselves to be conformed to worldly purposes and standards. Romans 12:2 assumes that is already happening and directs us to bring the conforming process to a halt. The Greek verb translated "conform" (*sunschēmatizō*) refers to the act of assuming an outward appearance that does not accurately reflect what is within. The addition of the prefix *sun* implies that the expression is patterned after a definite model. Paul is saying, "Don't masquerade as if you belong to the world; that would be patterning yourself inconsistently with who you really are." It is inconceivable that Christians would want to wear the mask of the world, but many do.

Greek scholar Kenneth Wuest paraphrased Paul's thought in these words: "Stop assuming an outward expression which is patterned after this world, an expression which does not come from, nor is it representative of what you are in your inner being as a regenerated child of God" (*Wuest's Word Studies from the Greek New Testament*, vol. 1 [Grand Rapids, Mich.: Eerdmans, 1955], pp. 206-7).

B. A Positive Transformation (v. 2*b*)

"Be ye transformed by the renewing of your mind."

1. The meaning

   The root of the Greek verb here translated "transformed" gives us the English word *metamorphosis*. It indicates a total change. We're to change our outward appearance to match what we are within. It's used in Matthew 17:2 of Jesus' transfiguration, when His outward human appearance changed to reflect the divine glory within. We are to be transformed on the outside to match what our redeemed selves are like on the inside. Since the verb is a present passive imperative, the verse could be paraphrased, "Stop allowing yourself to be conformed to the world, and start allowing yourself to be continually transformed."

2. The method

   a) The Spirit of God

      Second Corinthians 3:18 tells us that transformation is ultimately the work of the Spirit. He changes us from one level of glory to the next, conforming us to the image of Christ. He accomplishes that work in us by the renewing of the mind. The Greek word translated "renewing" here conveys the idea of renovation.

b) The Word of God

A Christian renovates his mind by knowing the Word of God and applying it to his life.

(1) Psalm 119:11—David said, "Thy Word have I hidden in mine heart, that I might not sin against thee." If you're going to walk worthy of the life to which God has called you, you've got to know the Word of God.

(2) Colossians 1:28—Paul stated the principle of "teaching every man in all wisdom, that we may present every man perfect in Christ Jesus." A perfect life comes out of perfect knowledge.

(3) Colossians 3:10—Paul said, "Put on the new man, that is renewed in knowledge."

(4) Colossians 3:16—Paul said to "let the word of Christ dwell in you richly."

The renewed mind is a mind saturated and controlled by the Word of God. Do you spend as much time in the Word of God as you do in the allurements of the world? Have you "set your affection on things above, not on things on the earth" (Col. 3:2)? When something unexpected happens in your life, is your involuntary response biblical? If it is, that's a good sign that you have a renewed mind and are preoccupied with the Word of God. Only a person with a renewed mind can resist conformity to the world and present his body to God.

IV. PRESENTING YOUR WILL TO GOD (v. 2*c*)

"That ye may prove what is that good, and acceptable, and perfect, will of God."

When we've presented our souls, bodies, and minds to God, we will acknowledge God's will as being good, acceptable, and perfect. We will abandon our imperfect plans and seek God's will as our top priority. We will want to do what God wants to accomplish in and through us. Where we live or what we possess won't matter so much anymore.

A renewed mind goes along with a submissive will housed in a body presented as a living sacrifice. It all comes in one package. You can't present your body unless you have a renewed mind because you won't have the will to do it.

Submission to God's will is not something you do once in your life. It is done every waking moment by the conscious renewing of your mind. Some people hesitate to follow God's will and pursue their own instead. But you never need to fear the will of God because it is good, acceptable, and perfect.

Conclusion

The renewed mind, the submissive will, and the consecrated body go along with the redeemed soul. The process of becoming more like Christ is not a complicated procedure. The fact that a Christian's response to eleven chapters of God's redeeming work could be distilled down to simple principles contained in two verses proves it.

Chinese mystic Watchman Nee ended his book *The Normal Christian Life* ([Wheaton, Ill.: Tyndale, 1957], pp. 283-4) with these words:

"I always like to think of the words of that 'great woman' of Shunem. Speaking of the prophet, whom she had observed but whom she did not know very well, she said, 'Behold now, I perceive that this is an holy man of God which passeth by us continually' (2 Kings 4:9). It was not what Elisha said or did that conveyed that impression, but what he was. By his merely passing by she could detect something. . . . What are people sensing about us? We may leave many kinds of impressions. We may leave the impression that we are clever, that we are gifted, that we are this or that or the other. But no, the impression left by Elisha was an impression of God.

"This matter of our impact upon others turns upon one thing, and that is the working of the Cross in us with regard to the pleasure of the heart of God. It demands that I seek his pleasure, that I seek to satisfy him only, and I do not mind how much it costs me to do so. . . . There must be something—a willingness to yield, a breaking and a pouring out of everything to him—which gives release to that fragrance of Christ and produces in other lives an awareness of need, drawing them out and on to know the Lord. This is what I feel to be the heart of everything. The Gospel has as its one object the producing in us sinners of a condition that will satisfy the heart of our God. In order that he may have that, we come to him with all we have, all we are—yes, even the most cherished things in our spiritual experience—and we make known to him: 'Lord, I am willing to let go all of this for you; not just for your work, not for your children, not for anything else at all, but altogether and only for yourself!' Oh to be wasted! It is a blessed thing to be wasted for the Lord!"

Focusing on the Facts

1. What do some people wrongly believe to be the key to spiritual victory? What is the real key (see p. 9)?
2. What are some kinds of spiritual sacrifices a Christian can offer? What is the supreme act of spiritual worship (see p. 10)?
3. Why do many Christians not render the service that is due God (see p. 10)?
4. Was an Old Testament believer exempt from being a living sacrifice? Support your answer with Scripture (see pp. 10-11).
5. What does Paul's addressing his Roman audience as "brethren" imply about who can make a proper offering to God (see p. 12)?
6. Why did the Macedonian Christians give to others so sacrificially (2 Cor. 8:5; see p. 12)?
7. Does the fact that a person may immediately respond in joy to the truth about Christ mean he is saved? Support your answer using the parable of the sower (see p. 13).
8. What is the basis for Paul's entreaty to dedicate our lives to God (see p. 13)?
9. Explain the significance of explaining doctrine before requiring duty (see pp. 15-16).
10. Why isn't it always easy to yield our bodies to God's will (see p. 16)?
11. According to Romans 8:23, what do our bodies still await (see p. 17)?

12. What is the natural result of concluding that the body is of no consequence? Cite Scripture that counters that low view of the body (see pp. 18-19).
13. Compare the living sacrifice Paul mentioned with the animal sacrifices under the Mosaic system (see p. 19).
14. How did the New Testament enhance the Greek word translated "holy" (see p. 21)?
15. According to Malachi 1:7-8, what was the evidence that the Israelites had compromised their devotion to God (see p. 21)?
16. Describe the spiritual worship that is acceptable or reasonable to God (see p. 22)?
17. Why should we not allow ourselves to be conformed to this world (see p. 23)?
18. Explain how Christians can be transformed. Support your answer with Scripture (see pp. 24-25).
19. A renewed mind goes along with what (see p. 26)?

Pondering the Principles

1. The psalmist asked, "What shall I render unto the Lord for all his benefits toward me?" (Ps. 116:12). Ponder the list of God's mercies on pages 13-14 and reflect on how the Lord has worked personally in your life. How would you answer the question of the psalmist?

2. Reread David Livingstone's comments on page 20. Why do you believe he did not see the living sacrifice he made as being a sacrifice? Are you convinced that the best the world offers will be greatly overshadowed by the glory to be revealed in and for us in heaven? Meditate on Hebrews 11:24-26 and Philippians 3 to strengthen your eternal perspective.

3. Would you consider your life a living sacrifice offered to God? Although you may not be working in a full-time Christian ministry, have you set apart your life to honor Him in everything you do? Do you serve God wholeheartedly with pure motives? Are you giving Him the best of your time and talents or only what is convenient and left over? Strengthen the quality of your spiritual worship by daily renewing your mind as you submit your will to the Holy Spirit and the study of God's Word. As you do that you will find that your responses to varying situations in your life will be biblical and well-pleasing to the Lord.

2
Ministry of Spiritual Gifts—Part 1

Outline

Introduction
A. The Substitutes for the Savior
B. The Sacrifice of Serving
    1. A source of blessing
    2. A clarification on giftedness

Lesson
I. The Proper Attitude (v. 3)
    A. The Exhortation (v. 3*a*)
        1. The expression of humility
        2. The explanation of humility
            a) Proper thinking
                (1) Galatians 6:3
                (2) 1 Peter 5:5-6
            b) Improper thinking
                (1) Using a prominent gift boastfully
                (2) Depreciating a gift's value out of false humility
                (3) Counterfeiting a prominent gift
                (4) Failing to use an inconspicuous gift out of jealousy
                (5) Failing to use your gifts at all
    B. The Enablement (v. 3*b*)
        1. Divine sovereignty
            a) No gift should be sought after
            b) No gift should be left unused
        2. Divine sufficiency
II. The Proper Relationships (vv. 4-5)
    A. Diversity in the Body of Christ (v. 4)
    B. Unity in the Body of Christ (v. 5)

Introduction

A. The Substitutes for the Savior

The work of Jesus Christ in the world is our work—He has no hands but our hands, no feet but our feet, no voice but our voice. His ministry is committed to us. The work of the kingdom depends on our usefulness and faithfulness. To us who are redeemed—who have received the mercies of God as indicated in the first eleven chapters of Romans, been freed from the bondage of sin, and called children of God and saints of the Most High—is committed the task of being the hands, feet, and voice of the Lord Jesus Christ.

B. The Sacrifice of Serving

1. A source of blessing

Our service will not be effective or blessed by God unless we have first offered ourselves as living sacrifices. That involves giving up all that we are for His service. A living sacrifice is not something mystical or monastic. It is simply a determination to become useful to God. If you claim to have given yourself wholly to God yet aren't ministering effectively in some capacity, you have not truly given yourself to God. Service to God has meaning and results in blessing only when it is the outflow of total commitment. And only total commitment will produce effective service. The two go together.

There are many people who believe they have made a complete commitment to Christ but who offer evidence of no meaningful, God-blessed ministry in their lives. Rather than being driven with a passion to serve, they are driven with the desire to indulge their own needs and desires.

Some people who are involved in church activities can actually be lacking in spiritual devotion. Mere participation is not necessarily a sign of one's sincerity of commitment. I received a letter from a man who said, "Please meet with me and pray with me. I've driven my wife away because I taught her by example how to be a

Sunday saint yet live any way you want all week long. And then when things started to fall apart in our marriage, and I tried to call us to prayer and Bible reading, she thought it was another one of my facades. I have outwardly lived as a Christian and have been active in the church, but the rest of the time I lived a lie."

Superficial commitment without service is not acceptable to God. However, there can still be results from the ministry of a person who attempts to serve God without being committed to Him. When you're serving Him just because you like to see yourself doing it, feel good doing it, or know that others think well of you when you do it, good may still result. That is because the truth is so much more powerful than your limitations. But improper motives will cause you to forfeit any reward you might otherwise have received for your efforts. If God can get His message out through a clogged vessel, think how much more effective it could be if the vessel were clean (cf. Phil. 1:15-18; 2 Tim. 2:20-21). Every one of us who has come to Jesus Christ is called to make a supreme dedication to Him. Paul is addressing all Christians in Romans 12 (as the first four verses make clear), so no one is left out.

2. A clarification on giftedness

Paul describes spiritual gifts in Romans 12:3-8, but you will never know which ones you have or how to use them to their potential until you live out Romans 12:1-2. We need to commit ourselves totally to God and not hold back. Like the human brain, which it is said we use at a level far below its potential, many Christians aren't operating at full capacity because they're not completely yielding to God. When believers commit themselves to fully serving God, they will be achieving greater spiritual potential and be able to see their gifts operating in their fullness.

When I was in seminary I used to wonder how I could ever make it through, let alone spend my life teaching the Word of God and writing books and commentaries. But as I began to see God wanting more and more of my life, and as I progressively yielded more of it to Him, the

Spirit of God gave me greater opportunities for ministry. To have an effective ministry you don't need great intellectual capability or a dynamic personality; you need only make the commitment to be everything God wants you to be, whatever the cost. If you do, you will find your capabilities expanding to fulfill the ministries to which the Spirit of God directs you. Many people have trouble identifying their gifts and areas of ministry because they've never first fulfilled Romans 12:1-2 in their own lives, so they have only a limited amount of data with which to work.

Our usefulness to God depends on three things: proper attitude, proper relationships, and proper service.

Lesson

I. THE PROPER ATTITUDE (v. 3)

"For I say, through the grace given unto me, to every man that is among you, not to think of himself more highly than he ought to think, but to think soberly, according as God hath dealt to every man the measure of faith."

What is the proper attitude of one who is totally given over to God? An attitude of humility. "For" functions as a transition from the dedication spoken of in verses 1-2. Paul is emphasizing the issue of service. Romans 12:1-2 states the prerequisite for service. The right attitude for service begins when one surrenders himself to God's will. To make his point, Paul warns against the wrong attitude of pride.

A. The Exhortation (v. 3a)

"I say, through the grace given unto me, to every man that is among you, not to think of himself more highly than he ought to think, but to think soberly."

1. The expression of humility

Paul was not talking about saving grace, which is experienced by all believers. He is referring to the specific grace of his calling to be an apostle, for it was the grace of God that ordained him to that position. He received that call when Christ confronted him on the Damascus road (Acts 9:1-6; 26:9-20). Notice that Paul didn't begin his instructions by flaunting his authority as an apostle of Jesus Christ. In a verse on humility it would have been inappropriate for him to pull rank. He was humble even in the way he referred to his apostleship. He admitted he had the authority of Christ, but he knew it was given to him not because he was worthy but because Christ was gracious. In 1 Timothy 1:12-15 Paul says, "I thank Christ Jesus, our Lord, who hath enabled me, in that he counted me faithful, putting me into the ministry, who was before a blasphemer, and a persecutor, and injurious; but I obtained mercy. . . . And the grace of our Lord was exceedingly abundant with faith and love which is in Christ Jesus. This is a faithful saying, and worthy of all acceptance, that Christ Jesus came into the world to save sinners, of whom I am chief."

2. The explanation of humility

   a) Proper thinking

   Paul directly addressed all professing Christians at the church in Rome (and all others by implication) not to be proud in their perception of themselves. There are four forms of the Greek verb translated "to think" (*phroneō*) in that one statement. We could substitute the word *think* with *estimate* to paraphrase the verse as follows: "Don't overestimate yourself beyond a true estimate, but estimate yourself with a proper estimate." "To think soberly" (Gk., *sōphroneō*) refers to being in one's right mind. Conceit is treated as a form of insanity. If you overestimate yourself you're deluded about who you really are and what your capabilities and gifts are. This is the sin of exaggerated self-esteem. The Bible clearly states that the Lord hates a proud heart.

   (1) Galatians 6:3—"If a man think himself to be something, when he is nothing, he deceiveth himself."

(2) 1 Peter 5:5-6—"Be clothed with humility; for God resisteth the proud, and giveth grace to the humble. Humble yourselves, therefore, under the mighty hand of God, that he may exalt you in due time."

b) Improper thinking

We are to think rightly about ourselves. However, that doesn't mean we are to think ill of ourselves. Don't say, "I am a worm." That's false humility. When someone compliments you, don't brush off the compliment and claim that your accomplishment was nothing; that's a manipulative way of begging for more praise. Rather, think rightly by recognizing your limits and keeping a proper measure of your gifts. Don't overestimate or underestimate your gifts and abilities. Both are unacceptable.

The church in Corinth was having problems with right attitudes toward spiritual gifts. We learn from 1 Corinthians 12-14 that some of the Corinthians were selfishly longing to have the showy gifts. Some were trying to elevate themselves beyond what God had called them to do. They had the mind-set of Diotrephes, who sought preeminence within his church (3 John 9). James addressed the problem when he told his readers not to be so eager to be teachers because of the great responsibility involved (3:1). Settle for the gifts God has given you. Don't overestimate them, but don't underestimate them either.

Here are five wrong attitudes toward spiritual gifts:

(1) Using a prominent gift boastfully

When you use a prominent gift boastfully you think more highly of yourself than you ought to. That's the pompous use of a genuine gift. You want the whole world to know you're good at what you do, so you continually draw attention to yourself and promote your own causes. You have the feeling that you're superior to everyone else and have no need of them. That is the rea-

34

soning Paul characterizes in 1 Corinthians 12:21: "The eye cannot say unto the hand, I have no need of thee; nor again the head to the feet, I have no need of you."

(2) Depreciating a gift's value out of false humility

Some know they have prominent gifts that are unique or especially effective but play the game of false humility to receive greater praise. I had to deal with that early in my ministry when people would compliment my sermons or mention that my messages had been instrumental in their salvation. Rather than claim they were nothing and that I could have done better, I learned simply to say thank you and praise God for using me to bless others.

(3) Counterfeiting a prominent gift

Although you may not have a prominent gift, you may pretend that you do, trying to be what you're not. Just as a foot cannot perform the function of a head (1 Cor. 12:21), it would be wrong to seek another gift so that people could take more notice of you. You must recognize that God did not design the church so that everyone would be apostles, prophets, and teachers or have the gifts of miracles, healing, and tongues (1 Cor. 12:29-30). Rather than coveting the showy gifts, as did the Corinthians, and producing a counterfeit, be content with the gifts you have been given.

(4) Failing to use an inconspicuous gift out of jealousy

If you have a behind-the-scenes gift such as showing mercy, it would be wrong for you to ignore your gift because you are jealous of someone else's gift. That would be just as disastrous as if a foot said, "Because I am not a hand I am not going to have anything to do with the body" (cf. 1 Cor. 12:15).

35

(5) Failing to use your gifts at all

Paul says in Romans 12:6-8, "Having then gifts differing according to the grace that is given to us, whether prophecy, let us prophesy according to the proportion of faith; or ministry, let us wait on our ministering; or he that teacheth, on teaching; or he that exhorteth, on exhortation; he that giveth, let him do it with liberality; he that ruleth, with diligence; he that showeth mercy, with cheerfulness." We're to put our gifts to good use.

Whatever your gifts are, use them. Don't play games with your ego. Don't overestimate yourself and boast. Don't underestimate yourself and pretend to be humble. Those kinds of attitudes devastate the Body of Christ. We need a balanced view of our gifts.

Humility is not an overestimation, nor is it underestimation—it is an accurate estimation. It is being able to say, "Yes, God has gifted me. He's given me a way to serve Him for His glory. And He deserves all the credit." Just as Paul was not afraid to admit he was an apostle of Jesus Christ by God's grace, I am not afraid to say God has given me gifts of communicating the Word of God by His grace.

Some of you may believe your spiritual gifts are unimportant, but they are an integral part to the proper functioning of the Body of Christ. Just as the less beautiful organs of the body are often more necessary, so it is with spiritual gifts. Although you could do without an attractive nose, you couldn't do without a heart, which is very unattractive by comparison. So we want to estimate things the way God does instead of misestimating our way.

B. The Enablement (v. 3b)

"According as God hath dealt to every man the measure of faith."

1. Divine sovereignty

Whatever gift you have, God has given it to you. I don't function entirely the way I do in the Lord's work because I went to seminary but because I have been gifted by God. I want to do all I can to refine and sharpen those gifts, but how He has sovereignly gifted me ultimately determines how I serve Him. That makes my life a stewardship. It is therefore important that I give myself totally to Him since He has given me a gift to use for His glory in the advance of His kingdom. If you're ever to see the maximum potential of the gifts God has given to you, then start by giving your whole self to Him. He will maximize them by His own sovereign design.

The phrase "according as God hath dealt to every man" conveys some important things that we need to remember:

a) No gift should be sought after

All gifts are sovereignly given by God. Paul says in 1 Corinthians 12, "The manifestation of the Spirit is given to every man. . . . All these [gifts] worketh that one and the very same Spirit, dividing to every man severally as he will" (vv. 7-11). The Holy Spirit is the divine source of all spiritual gifts. The Greek word translated "severally" (*idios*) basically means "uniquely" or "individually." Because our gifts have been tailor-made by God to suit us, we should not be seeking after gifts. (Although some find support for seeking gifts in 1 Corinthians 12:31, I believe that verse should be translated as a statement of what the Corinthians were actually doing rather than as Paul's imperative to "covet earnestly the best gifts." The Greek text allows for such a translation, and the context and connotation of the verb translated "covet earnestly" practically require it.)

b) No gift should be left unused

Every gift is given by God for His own glory and for the advance of His kingdom. In 1 Corinthians 12:17-18 Paul says, "If the whole body were an eye, where were the hearing? If the whole were hearing, where were the smelling? But now hath God set the members, every one of them, in the body, as it hath pleased him." God has placed you in the Body according to His pleasure, and every gifted believer is necessary for the Body to function properly. Therefore we shouldn't depreciate the importance of any gift.

2. Divine sufficiency

Verse 3 is qualified by the phrase "the measure of faith." That implies that the measure for everyone is different. It's as though believers are cups that God has filled with different amounts and types of liquids. To put it another way, we are spiritual snowflakes—there aren't any two of us exactly alike. Although many Christians may have the same gift or gifts, our expression of them is unique.

The kind of faith Paul is speaking about is not saving faith, because that isn't measured out differently to everyone. Saving faith, which is the act of putting one's complete trust in the Person and work of the Lord Jesus Christ, isn't in the context of Romans 12. Rather, Paul is referring to the kind of faith it takes to operate our gifts. So if you have the gift of teaching and preaching, God will give you the faith required to use that gift—the necessary spiritual insight, capacity, and comprehension.

When we have a right estimation of our spiritual gifts and the divine capabilities that go along with them, we will be humble because we realize that we had nothing to do in selecting the gifts God gave us.

How Can I Know What My Gifts Are?

1. Present yourself to God as a living sacrifice (Rom. 12:1-2).
2. Know that you're gifted (Rom. 12:3).
3. Pray for wisdom (James 1:5).
4. Don't seek for a particular gift (Acts 8:18-20).
5. Examine your heart's desires (Ps. 37:4).
6. See what others commend you for (Acts 6:1-6).
7. Review where God seems to bless your ministry (Acts 14:27).
8. Serve with your whole heart (1 Chron. 28:9).
9. Cultivate your gifts as they become obvious to you (1 Pet. 4:10-11).

When you've done all that, you will probably find it impossible to precisely label your gift, although you might have a general idea what it is. I can't tell you exactly what my gift is. Sometimes I preach the gospel, sometimes I teach the Bible, and sometimes I exhort people to live by biblical principles. But all those activities put together is my gift. I know other people who preach, teach, and exhort, but those gifts are expressed differently in their ministries. I believe that a spiritual gift consists of areas of giftedness that God has blended together to make a believer what he is. A spiritual gift is like the blending of different colors of paint on a artist's palette to paint a portrait. That's what God did when He made you for spiritual service. You are a composite of a variety of gifts, some of which may be more dominant than others. That is why you may find it difficult to have a clear definition of your gift.

II. THE PROPER RELATIONSHIPS (vv. 4-5)

A. Diversity in the Body of Christ (v. 4)

"As we have many members in one body, and all members have not the same office."

Paul uses his famous metaphor of the physical body to illustrate the working of a church. He points out that the body has many parts—a head, eyes, nose, mouth, ears, teeth, arms, legs, fingers, toes, and internal organs—but that they don't have the same function. The analogy of the body beautifully illustrates the relationship of individual believers to the whole. We constitute one Body, yet we work in different capacities that complement one another.

B. Unity in the Body of Christ (v. 5)

"So we, being many, are one body in Christ, and every one members one of another."

Like a human body whose parts work together, believers form a spiritual Body, sharing common life, gifts, ministry, resources, joy, and sorrow. Paul emphasizes our unity in this verse. Yet at the same time we are all diverse.

If one part of your body is not functioning, you've got a problem. Everything in the body has to work together for the body as a whole to work properly. Likewise, everyone in the church has to work together or the rest of the church suffers. Because each believer has something unique to offer, if we don't do what we were gifted to do, the Body of Christ is crippled. As unified diversity is characteristic of the human body, so is it characteristic of the church.

Focusing on the Facts

1. How is the work of Jesus Christ in the world to be accomplished (see p. 30)?
2. What must we first do before our service to God can be effective and blessed by Him (see pp. 32-33)?
3. Explain how it is possible for some people to be involved in a church but lacking in spiritual dedication (see pp. 30-31).
4. Can there be good results when we serve God with the wrong motives? Explain (see p. 31).
5. What is the proper attitude of one who is totally committed to serving God (Rom. 12:3; see p. 32)?
6. What kind of grace is Paul referring to in Romans 12:3 (see pp. 32-33)?
7. How are we warned not to think about ourselves? Does that imply that we should think ill of ourselves? Explain (see p. 34).
8. Explain the wrong attitudes that lead Christians to counterfeit prominent gifts or fail to use inconspicuous ones (see pp. 34-36).
9. God has given us gifts to use for His _____ and the advance of His _____ (see p. 37).
10. What does the fact that gifts are sovereignly given by God imply about seeking them (see p. 37)?
11. Explain how believers are like spiritual snowflakes (see p. 38).
12. Why can it be difficult to precisely determine what one's spiritual gifts are (see p. 39)?
13. What two contrasting qualities are characteristic of the Body of Christ (see pp. 39-40)?

Pondering the Principles

1. A balanced view of humility is difficult to maintain. Many Christians believe it is pious to underestimate their worth. Converse-

ly, there's a philosophy being promoted today that is preoccupied with self-esteem. As is often the case with extremes, both positions are unbiblical. Memorize 1 Peter 5:5-6 to help keep you in check: "All of you, clothe yourselves with humility toward one another, for God is opposed to the proud, but gives grace to the humble. Humble yourselves, therefore, under the mighty hand of God, that He may exalt you at the proper time" (NASB).

2. Do you know your area of giftedness? If not, look over the steps listed on page 38 to help you start the process of determining it. If you are not currently involved in a ministry, start ministering to others in an area that interests you and that you feel qualified in. Then look for the confirmation of God's blessing and the encouragement of other believers.

3
Ministry of Spiritual Gifts—Part 2

Outline

Introduction
A. A Case of Inactivity
B. A Cause of Ineffectiveness
   1. The devastation of selfishness
   2. The importance of sacrificial service

Review
  I. The Proper Attitude (v. 3)
 II. The Proper Relationships (vv. 4-5)

Lesson
III. The Proper Service (vv. 6-8)
  A. Spiritual Gifts Discussed (v. 6*a*)
    1. The categories of spiritual gifts
     a) The temporary sign gifts
      (1) Their purpose
       (*a*) 2 Corinthians 12:12
       (*b*) Hebrews 2:4
       (*c*) Mark 16:20
      (2) Their passing
     b) The permanent edifying gifts
    2. The variation of spiritual gifts
     a) The Greek words
     b) The gift lists
  B. Spiritual Gifts Defined (vv. 6*b*-8)
    1. Prophecy/preaching (v. 6*b*)
     a) Explained
     b) Exemplified
     c) Exhorted

2. Serving (v. 7*a*)
    a) Explained
    b) Exemplified
3. Teaching (v. 7*b*)
    a) Explained
    b) Exemplified

Introduction

A. A Case of Inactivity

I read about a man in Saskatchewan, Canada, who has a hobby of collecting rare violins. Unfortunately, many violins in his collection aren't likely to be used. Wouldn't it be marvelous if the great violinists of the world were able to play beautiful music on those violins? Some churches are similar to that man's collection of unused violins: they are a collection of gifted Christians, but none of them are making any music, so to speak. They're merely on display, waiting to be played. Some of their gifts have been enhanced with Bible school or college training or previous ministerial experience. But they remain unused. They have become museum pieces.

B. A Cause of Ineffectiveness

1. The devastation of selfishness

Some people identify Grace Church as John MacArthur's church. That isn't so. Grace Church is the church of Jesus Christ, whether I'm around or not. No individual can claim that a church is his, because an effective church requires a high degree of dependence and mutual loyalty among its members. The Body of Christ needs to focus on those things. But that isn't easy in our society because it's fixed on selfishly pampering itself. It's little wonder that our society has such tremendous problems with mental illness, because selfish people generally are the kind who are mentally ill. William Kirk Kilpatrick, professor of educational psychology at Boston College and a graduate of Harvard University, has written a book entitled *Psychological Seduction: The Failure of*

Modern Psychology (Nashville: Nelson, 1983). In it he says, "Extreme forms of mental illness are always extreme cases of self-absorption. . . . The distinctive quality, the thing that literally sets paranoid people apart, is hyper self-consciousness" (p. 67). So if you become excessively absorbed with yourself, it can lead to paranoia.

2. The importance of sacrificial service

Christian theologians, long before psychologists had anything to say, dealt with the devastating effects of selfishness. St. Augustine, a fourth-century church Father, wrote, "Two cities have been formed by two loves; the earthly by the love of self, even to the contempt of God, the heavenly by the love of God, even to the contempt of self. The former, in a word, glories in itself, the latter in the Lord" (*The City of God* 14:28).

Sixteenth-century reformer John Calvin said, "For so blindly do we all rush in the direction of self-love that everyone thinks he has a good reason for exalting himself and despising all others in comparison." He then offered a cure for that problem in the church: "There is no other remedy than to pluck up by the roots those most noxious pests, self-love and love of victory. . . . This the doctrine of Scripture does. For it teaches us to remember, that the endowments which God has bestowed upon us are not our own, but His free gifts, and that those who plume themselves upon them betray their ingratitude" (*Institutes of the Christian Religion*, 2 vols. [Grand Rapids: Eerdmans, 1966], 2:10).

Facing the same problem in the community to which he wrote, the author of Hebrews said, "Let us consider how to stimulate one another to love and good deeds, not forsaking our own assembling together" (Heb. 10:24-25, NASB). That is a call for a ministry of self-sacrifice.

Review

Ministry begins when you present your body to God as a living sacrifice, submitting your mind and will to God. Out of that flows the right use of spiritual gifts. If we are to use the gifts God has given us in interdependent and sacrificial ministry to one another, we must focus on three things:

I. THE PROPER ATTITUDE (v. 3; see pp. 32-39)

"I say, through the grace given unto me, to every man that is among you, not to think of himself more highly than he ought to think, but to think soberly, according as God hath dealt to every man the measure of faith."

We are to be humble, possessing an accurate assessment of our giftedness and a grateful heart for God's gifts to us. We do not exaggerate our function, nor do we undervalue its worth. God has designed each of us uniquely to function within the Body of Christ. If we fail to have the proper attitude of humility, we will become frustrated in our spiritual growth and ineffective in our ministry.

II. THE PROPER RELATIONSHIPS (vv. 4-5; see pp. 39-40)

"As we have many members in one body, and all members have not the same office, so we, being many, are one body in Christ, and every one members one of another."

Just as there are many parts to the body, so the church, the Body of Christ, is composed of members having differing functions and gifts. As the body is one and yet has multifaceted functions, so the church is one and yet has many members. Within its unity there is diversity. Our spiritual gifts are the God-given channels through which the Holy Spirit builds up the church (1 Cor. 14:12).

Lesson

III. THE PROPER SERVICE (vv. 6-8)

"Having then gifts differing according to the grace that is given to us, whether prophecy, let us prophesy according to the proportion of faith; or ministry, let us wait on our ministering; or he that teacheth, on teaching; or he that exhorteth, on exhortation; he that giveth, let him do it with liberality; he that ruleth, with diligence; he that showeth mercy, with cheerfulness."

A. Spiritual Gifts Discussed (v. 6a)

Paul's approach in Romans 12 is an exhortation to use the gifts, not a rebuke for misusing them as was the case in the Corinthian church. He wanted the Roman Christians to first present themselves to the Lord and rightly evaluate what God had given them to do as members of the Body and then use the gifts they had been given.

As members of the Body of Christ we depend on the interchange that occurs between us. That involves using our gifts to serve one another. In verses 6-8 Paul mentions these gifts: prophecy (preaching), serving, teaching, exhorting, giving, leading, and showing mercy.

1. The categories of spiritual gifts

Spiritual gifts fall into three categories in the New Testament: sign gifts, speaking gifts, and serving gifts. The apostle Peter is responsible for the designation of the latter two (1 Pet. 4:10-11). They can be grouped together as permanent or ongoing edifying gifts, in contrast to the temporary sign gifts.

a) The temporary sign gifts

(1) Their purpose

These gifts were intended to serve as signs pointing to something significant. They were unique to the time of the apostles as the church of the New Covenant was being established. They authenti-

47

cated the teaching of the apostles and the subsequent writing of Scripture.

(a) 2 Corinthians 12:12—Paul specifically identified sign gifts as those belonging to an apostle: "Truly the signs of an apostle were wrought among you in all patience, in signs, and wonders, and mighty deeds." The miraculous sign gifts include tongues (languages), the interpretation of tongues, healing, and miracles.

(b) Hebrews 2:4—As the apostles were preaching the gospel, God was "bearing them witness, with signs and wonders, and with diverse miracles, and gifts of the Holy Spirit."

(c) Mark 16:20—The apostles "went forth, and preached everywhere, the Lord working with them, and confirming the word with signs following." Miraculous gifts attended the works of the apostles so people would know they were from God. There was no New Testament with which to compare their teachings, so it was the miracles that authenticated the message and the messengers.

(2) Their passing

The sign gifts are delineated in 1 Corinthians 12. Paul wrote his first epistle to the Corinthians around A.D. 54. The book of Romans was written four years later. It is intriguing that Paul's list of spiritual gifts in 1 Corinthians is unlike his list of gifts in Romans, for none of the miraculous sign gifts are mentioned in the latter. However, they were much a part of the list of 1 Corinthians a few years earlier. In the book of Ephesians, which was written around A.D. 63, Paul talks about spiritual gifts in chapter 4 but again neglects to mention the sign gifts. And Peter's first epistle, written around A.D. 66, doesn't mention the sign gifts in the section on spiritual gifts in his fourth chapter.

48

It appears that the sequence of New Testament books reveals a diminishing use of the sign gifts. When they passed away with the apostles, that left the speaking and serving gifts: "As every man hath received the gift, even so minister the same one to another, as good stewards of the manifold grace of God. If any man speak, let him speak as the oracles of God; if any man minister [serve], let him do it as of the ability which God giveth, that God in all things may be glorified through Jesus Christ" (1 Pet. 4:10-11). Again nothing is said about sign gifts, which were unique to the early apostolic era.

b) The permanent edifying gifts

The speaking gifts include prophecy, teaching, and exhortation; the serving gifts include serving, giving, leading, and showing mercy. Furthermore, Paul's instruction to the Roman Christians does not include the sign gifts because the church at Rome did not have the same problem the Corinthian church had of counterfeiting and abusing them.

2. The variation of spiritual gifts

a) The Greek words

In 1 Corinthians 12 spiritual gifts are designated by the Greek word *pneumatikōn*, which means "spirituals" or "spiritual matters." In Romans 12 they are designated by *charismata*, meaning "grace gifts." Both refer to the spiritual gifts given by God, but each emphasizes a different aspect. The former refers to their being energized by the Holy Spirit. The latter refers to the graciousness of God.

b) The gift lists

Another variation between the lists of spiritual gifts in Romans 12 and 1 Corinthians 12 is which speaking and serving gifts they include. First Corinthians 12 adds the gifts of faith and discerning spirits. Romans 12 adds the gifts of exhorting, giving, and showing mercy. The gifts of teaching, ministry, and ruling are synonymous with the words of wisdom and knowledge, helps, and government in 1 Corinthians. Because the lists are somewhat different, we can conclude that they are not rigid, all-inclusive lists; there's a sense of flexibility and latitude. They are but samples of the dimensions of ministry within the Body of Christ. I consider them to be general categories of giftedness in which there could be many different variations. Christians with the gift of teaching would be distinct from others with the same gift because of the uniqueness of God's design. These general categories may be blended with other gifts to create a composite gift that is unique to us and hard to identify specifically.

Motivation for Ministry

If you are a Christian and are not ministering to others with your spiritual gift, then you need to reevaluate your priorities, epecially if your excuse is that you're too busy. Maybe you've forgotten the first eleven chapters of Romans—all that God has done for you. Our failure to use what God has given us for His glory must disappoint the One who made the supreme sacrifice by coming into the world to die on the cross for us. Such an ungrateful response indicates that you haven't presented yourself as a living sacrifice.

God isn't asking us to do something He hasn't equipped us to do, so there should be no excuse for not using our gifts. Although we could be motivated to serve God out of fear of judgment or peer pressure, such external means would not solve the internal problem—a lack of gratitude for the One who died for us.

B. Spiritual Gifts Defined (vv. 6b-8)

1. Prophecy/preaching (v. 6b)

a) Explained

The first of the seven gifts Paul mentions here is prophecy. This gift is often misunderstood. It is basically a gift of preaching or proclamation. Its use here does not refer to the apostolic gift of dispensing divine revelation, for that has ceased. Its inclusion in Romans 12 with other ongoing gifts of the church is good reason for us to believe it is a permanent edifying gift for today.

Prophecy is an important gift, so much so that the apostle Paul in writing to the Corinthians said more about it and the gift of tongues than any other gifts. The Greek verb *prophēteuō* refers to speaking out or making a pronouncement on a spiritual issue. It isn't extraordinary or supernatural in that sense and doesn't therefore have to imply foretelling the future or dispensing new revelation. It is simply referring to the public proclamation of Scripture.

The best definition of the prophetic gift is found in 1 Corinthians 14:3: "He that prophesieth speaketh unto men to edification, and exhortation, and comfort." Its purpose is to build up believers, challenge them to obedience, and comfort them in need. Similarly 1 Peter 4:11 says, "If any man speak, let him speak as of the oracles of God." Prophecy is a speaking gift that uses the Word of God for its content. It isn't necessarily foretelling the future by supernatural revelation. First Corinthians 14:24-25 indicates that both believers and unbelievers can be addressed by those with the gift of preaching or prophesying.

b) Exemplified

Throughout redemptive history God has had His spokesmen. Sometimes they gave new revelation, like the prophet Ezekiel, saying, "The word of the Lord came unto me" (Ezek. 7:1). That happened often in the Old Testament. But there were also times when what God's spokesmen were proclaiming wasn't new and direct revelation; they were preaching revelation that had already been received. Often you will find Old Testament prophets who instructed, exhorted, warned, rebuked, and encouraged. They called for obedience, repentance, reverence, righteousness, and they promised blessing. Their emphasis was on the practical application of God's

51

Word to the situation at hand. With the New Testament gift of prophecy you will find the same emphasis (cf. Acts 13:1, 5; 15:32).

John Calvin did not consider the gift of prophecy to be the gift of foretelling the future. He wrote, "I prefer, however, to follow those who understand the word in a wider sense to mean the peculiar gift of revelation by which a man performs the office of interpreter with skill and dexterity in expounding the will of God" (*The Epistles of Paul the Apostle to the Romans and to the Thessalonians* [Grand Rapids: Eerdmans, 1960], p. 269).

c) Exhorted

Paul exhorts those with the gift of prophecy to preach "according to the proportion of faith" (Rom 12:6). Some commentators suggest that the faith referred to here is objective in the sense of revealed truth and could therefore be translated as "according to the proportion of *the* faith." Jude referred to the body of Christian doctrine as "the faith which was once delivered unto the saints" (Jude 3). Or, the faith referred to here could be subjective and refer to the measure of personal faith God has given you (cf. Rom. 12:3). God has meted out to every Christian certain abilities and the faith to make use of them. Both interpretations make sense. So when you preach, make sure you use the Word of God, the basis of the Christian faith, and make sure your preaching is consistent with your abilities.

First Thessalonians 5 indicates that the gift of prophecy goes far beyond the revelatory gift that gradually ceased with the writing of the New Testament: "Quench not the Spirit. Despise not prophesyings. Prove all things; hold fast that which is good" (vv. 19-21). Those exhortations are interrelated. If you despise prophesying, you'll quench the Spirit. If you accept prophesying, then you must test it and make sure it's accurate. That can be done by comparing it with "the faith"—Scripture—or by determining if it exalts Jesus Christ (Rev. 19:10). All biblical preaching proclaims the Word of God and exalts the Son of God.

So Paul says that if you have the gift of prophecy, you're to use it to the full extent of the faith God has given you to proclaim the faith once delivered to the saints. That is what Paul exhorted Timothy to do in 2 Timothy 4:2-5: "Preach the word; be diligent in season, out of season; reprove, rebuke, exhort with all long-suffering and doctrine. For the time will come when they will not endure sound doctrine but, after their own lusts, shall they heap to themselves teachers, having itching ears; and they shall turn away their ears from the truth, and shall be turned unto fables. But watch thou in all things, endure afflictions, do the work of an evangelist, make full proof of thy ministry." That's part of Paul's message to the Romans.

The gift of prophecy may be manifested in a variety of degrees, from someone preaching to massive crowds to the street preacher who attracts a small audience. I pray for God to raise up more preachers with a passion for proclaiming His truth. As for myself, I am grateful to God that He has given me this gift and endeavor to be faithful to use it for His glory.

2. Serving (v. 7*a*)

   a) Explained

      The Greek word translated "ministry" is *diakonia*, from which the English words *deacon* and *deaconess* are derived. Believers who fill those offices in the church obviously have the gift of ministry. It is equivalent to what is referred to as "helps" (Gk., *antilēmpsis*, "support") in 1 Corinthians 12:28. The gift of ministry is a support gift of practical help or service.

      Although *diakonia* is translated "ministry" in verse 7, it does not always have a spiritual meaning; it was often used of those who wait upon the needs of others, as a waiter provides service to those who are dining. It was used of Peter's mother-in-law, who, after being healed by Jesus, arose and served those present (Luke 4:38-39). It's used several places in the New Testament for providing a meal (Luke 10:40) as well as in providing some kind of spiritual service (Eph. 4:12). It's a common word in the New Testament that is used more than seventy-five times for various dimensions of serving—from the official service of someone designated as a deacon or deaconess to the unofficial service of someone just stepping into a gap to serve.

b) Exemplified

In Acts 6 the apostles recognized their need to devote their time to preaching the Word and praying, so they requested the support of others who could carry out the task of serving tables (v. 2). Things haven't changed in that regard. The church is dependent on the helpers. If people with the gifts of helps or ministry don't use their gifts, the church has to find other people who will perform the basic but important tasks that keep a church functioning properly. Whether it's stuffing envelopes, making phone calls, cleaning things, visiting members in hospitals, or providing meals for those who need them, there are myriad supportive tasks that have to be done in the ministry. So if you have the gift of serving, your church needs you to serve. You have a practical gift that needs to be used.

3. Teaching (v. 7*b*)

a) Explained

The Greek word translated "teaching" is from the verb *didaskō*, which refers to systematic training. It's the kind of work a choir director does in training a choir over a period of time until finally it has mastered the music and is ready to perform. Preaching, on the other hand, refers to an urgent proclamation that is not intended to be repeated to the same audience. John the Baptist's message about the coming Messiah is an example of preaching.

Teaching involves the ongoing process of systematically taking people from one point to another. It can refer to a teacher in a seminary, a Sunday school teacher, or someone who disciples a person one-on-one. It is the ministry of leading someone to a greater understanding of God's Word. Acts 2:42 says that the early church "continued steadfastly in the apostles' doctrine." There was a didactic exercise going on to analyze and systematize the Word of God when the church came together. That's what we're called to do in a general sense in Matthew 28. Jesus said, "Go therefore and make disciples of all the nations . . . teaching them to observe all that I commanded you" (vv. 19-20, NASB).

b) Exemplified

It is clear that God gave the gift of teaching to Paul. Besides being divinely enabled to publicly proclaim truth at certain times, he was an excellent teacher. The epistle to the Romans alone shows his genius at systematically imparting truth. In 2 Timothy 1:11 he uses both words to describe himself: "I am appointed a preacher . . . and a teacher." It's not uncommon for a person to be both a preacher and a teacher in God's design.

I believe Timothy also was a teacher. In 2 Timothy 2:2 Paul says, "The things that thou hast from me among many witnesses, the same commit thou to faithful men, who shall be able to teach others also."

Jesus certainly had the ability to do that. Luke 24:27 tells us that as He walked on the road to Emmaus with two disciples "he expounded unto them, in all the scriptures, the things concerning himself." The Greek word translated "expounded" is from the verb *diermēneuō*. It is the word from which comes the English word *hermeneutics*, the science of interpreting Scripture.

I believe all elders are to have the gift of teaching. First Timothy 3:2 says that elders are to be "apt to teach." That's the ability to analyze the Word of God and instruct people in it. The primary function of a pastor is to interpret Scripture so it is understandable and then systematically instruct his congregation with it. It's not unusual for a pastor to be both a teacher and a preacher, but he must at least have the gift of teaching as a basic requirement for being an elder (1 Tim. 3:2). We need not expect that all men who are leading their churches have the ability to dynamically proclaim Christ as well as teach biblical truth. Although a pastor may speak publicly, he is not required to have the gift of prophecy. So a pastor who teaches and preaches is not the standard for all other pastors. God's gifts are different and unique. A pastor or an elder must be evaluated on the basis of whether he faithfully and systematically teaches the Word of God. Missiologist Eric Fife once said that if the study is a lounge, the pulpit is an impertinence. If you don't have the gift of teaching, please don't teach, because teachers of God's Word will be subject to greater condemnation because of their high level of responsibility and accountability (James 3:1).

You may be concluding that you're not a preacher or a teacher but only a server. That's fine. Serving is just as good as teaching or preaching. The issue isn't what your gift is; it's what you do with it. Your eternal commendation is not going to be whether you had the same effect that Billy Graham did on the world. Your eternal reward is going to be based on whether you maximized the gift God designed for you to use (cf. Matt. 25:14-30).

Focusing on the Facts

1. What trends in society make it difficult for Christians to depend on one another and maintain a mutual loyalty (see p. 44)?
2. Identify the vital interchange that must occur between the members of Christ's Body (see p. 47).
3. List the three categories of spiritual gifts. Under which broader classification can two of those categories be grouped (see p. 47)?
4. What are the sign gifts, and what was their purpose? Support your answer with Scripture (see pp. 47-48).

5. Explain the evidence of Scripture that supports the passing of sign gifts (see pp. 48-49).
6. Identify the speaking gifts and the serving gifts. What are two reasons that Paul did not include the sign gifts in his list of gifts in Romans 12 (see p. 49)?
7. What can we learn from the differences in the lists of gifts in Romans 12 and 1 Corinthians 12 (see pp. 49-50)?
8. If a Christian is not ministering to others, what may he need to do (see p. 50)?
9. Define the gift of prophecy. What is its purpose according to 1 Corinthians 14:3 (see pp. 50-51)?
10. Discuss what Paul might have meant by using the gift of prophecy "according to the measure of faith" (Rom. 12:6; see p. 52).
11. How does Paul imply that we can quench the Spirit (1 Thess. 5:19-20)? Does that mean we should accept every message? Explain (see pp. 52-53).
12. What is the reason for the urgency of Paul's exhortation to Timothy in 2 Timothy 4:2-5 (see p. 53)?
13. What gift do deacons and deaconesses usually have (see p. 53)?
14. Explain the gift of serving (see pp. 53-54).
15. What did the apostles request so that they could devote their time to studying the Word and praying (Acts 6:2-4; see p. 54)?
16. Describe the gift of teaching. How does it differ from preaching (see pp. 54-55)?
17. What should be the primary function of a pastor (see p. 56)?
18. Although a pastor may have both the gifts of preaching and teaching, which gift must he have as an elder, according to 1 Timothy 3:2 (see p. 56)?
19. How will our spiritual gifts be a factor in determining the extent of our eternal reward (see p. 56)?

Pondering the Principles

1. Our encouragement of those who are ministering to us can be instrumental in helping them determine their effectiveness and the proper use of their gifts. Have you recently encouraged your pastor, Sunday school teacher, or other fellow believer for the effect of his ministry in your life? Not only will you be confirming in his own heart that he is operating in God's will, but

you will be encouraging him to manifest even greater love and good deeds (Heb. 10:24-25).

2. Are you truly thankful for the gifts you have? Do you understand how essential they are to the Body of Christ? You don't need to wait for a formal invitation to minister to others. All you need to do is try to evaluate your gifts and make yourself available. Only then will you have the joy of knowing that you've made the most of your life. If you currently aren't demonstrating a willingness to use your gift, you're postponing God's blessing for being faithful with what He has entrusted to you. No matter how small your current ministry may be, it is the proving ground for your readiness to be given greater ministry opportunities. Jesus taught that our faithfulness in the little things would bring the privilege of having greater authority and responsibilities (Luke 16:10-12; 19:17-19). If you are not yet pursuing any ministry, begin today by committing yourself to the Lord as a living sacrifice to be used for His glory.

4
Ministry of Spiritual Gifts—Part 3

Outline

Review
 I. The Proper Attitude (v. 3)
 II. The Proper Relationships (vv. 4-5)
III. The Proper Service (vv. 6-8)
   A. Spiritual Gifts Discussed (v. 6a)
   B. Spiritual Gifts Defined (vv. 6b-8)
      1. Prophecy/preaching (v. 6b)
      2. Serving (v. 7a)
      3. Teaching (v. 7b)

Lesson
      4. Exhorting (v. 8a)
         a) Explained
         b) Exemplified
         c) Exhorted
      5. Giving (v. 8b)
         a) Explained
         b) Exemplified
         c) Exhorted
      6. Leading (v. 8c)
         a) Explained
         b) Exemplified
         c) Exhorted
      7. Showing mercy (v. 8d)
         a) Explained
         b) Exemplified
         c) Exhorted

Conclusion

Review

I. THE PROPER ATTITUDE (v. 3; see pp. 32-39)

"I say, through the grace given unto me, to every man that is among you, not to think of himself more highly than he ought to think, but to think soberly, according as God hath dealt to every man the measure of faith."

II. THE PROPER RELATIONSHIPS (vv. 4-5; see pp. 39-40)

"As we have many members in one body, and all members have not the same office, so we, being many, are one body in Christ, and every one members one of another."

III. THE PROPER SERVICE (vv. 6-8)

"Having then gifts differing according to the grace that is given to us, whether prophecy, let us prophesy according to the proportion of faith; or ministry, let us wait on our ministering; or he that teacheth, on teaching; or he that exhorteth, on exhortation; he that giveth, let him do it with liberality; he that ruleth, with diligence; he that showeth mercy, with cheerfulness."

A. Spiritual Gifts Discussed (v. 6a; see pp. 47-50)

Paul calls every believer to minister. There is no such thing as an obedient Christian who isn't ministering. So Paul encourages us to use the spiritual gifts we've been given. He lists seven categories of giftedness: prophesying, serving, teaching, exhorting, giving, leading, and showing mercy. Those are some of the areas in which the Lord has blended our gifts with our personalities, experiences, opportunities, and Bible knowledge, and with the measure of faith He has given us.

B. Spiritual Gifts Defined (vv. 6b-8)

1. Prophecy/preaching (v. 6b; see pp. 50-53)

2. Serving (v. 7a; see pp. 53-54)

3. Teaching (v. 7b; see pp. 54-56)

4. Exhorting (v. 8*a*)

   a) Explained

   Whereas prophecy proclaims the truth, serving puts the truth into action, and teaching systematizes it, exhorting calls for a right response to the truth. The Greek word translated "exhort" means "to encourage," "to strengthen," "to advise," or "to comfort." Some believe exhortation is synonymous with counseling. I'd say rather than being a gift, counseling is a process in which the gift of exhorting may operate. A counselor would certainly be more effective if he had that gift.

   b) Exemplified

   There are many ways that the gift of exhorting manifests itself. It could involve encouraging people to stop sinning and start living righteously, comforting people in times of trouble or sorrow, or helping them to trust more in the Lord and walk by faith, believing that He will work things out. Paul alluded to this gift when he exhorted the Thessalonians to "warn them that are unruly, encourage the fainthearted, support the weak" (1 Thess. 5:14).

   The gift of exhortation is the ministry of challenging God's people to act consistently with His will. If you're weak and defeated, then someone needs to come to you and say, "Let me encourage you to take your eyes off your problems and focus them on the Lord; be strong in the Lord and the power of His might. He is the victor, so there is no reason to be downhearted. Enjoy the victory that has been promised you." If you find someone in sorrow, you might gently encourage him by saying, "Why are you sorrowing as those who have no hope? Our God is a God of victory, and your sorrow will be turned some day into joy" (1 Thess. 4:13; 2 Cor. 7:9-10; John 16:20-22). If someone is fainthearted and afraid, you need to remind him that God is in control and that since no enemy is greater than He, His victory is guaranteed. The Lord not only is with us in the midst of troubles, but He can deliver us from them as well because He is our refuge and fortress (Ps. 91).

c) Exhorted

The Christian with the gift of exhortation leads people to live according to God's revelation. If exhortation is the area God has gifted you in, then use that gift. When you come across a situation in which you feel you must minister, that's probably the Spirit of God prompting your heart.

5. Giving (v. 8*b*)

a) Explained

The Greek word translated "give" in this verse is *metadidōmi*, which means "to impart one's earthly possessions to another." Although all Christians are called to give to the needs of others, some believers have the gift of giving with "liberality" (*haplotēs*, "simplicity"). It indicates a kind of giving that is single-minded—without having an ulterior motive. It implies giving for the glory of the Lord with no thought of regret or hope of repayment. Someone who gives with liberality is not interested in others taking notice of his generosity, unlike the Pharisees who gave to be seen by men (Matt. 6:1).

b) Exemplified

The Macedonians exemplified the practice of giving with liberality. And they gave that way in spite of their deep poverty, committing themselves first to doing the Lord's will and meeting the needs of others (2 Cor. 8:1-5).

In a similar manner the believers in the early church at Jerusalem sold what they had and distributed the proceeds to those in need (Acts 2:44-45; 4:34-37). When people made their pilgrimage to Jerusalem for the Feast of Pentecost, they would stay in the homes of the Jewish residents of the city. On the Day of Pentecost nearly three thousand people were saved (Acts 2:41), and we can assume that those who were from out of town didn't want to leave, because they had just been introduced into the community of those who worshiped Christ. Because of the Jerusalem church's willingness to support its rapidly growing membership, it became a model of generosity. Many of those who even sold their property had the gift of giving, for they were willing to do anything they could to share with those in need.

c) Exhorted

I thank God for those who have the gift of giving. If you have that gift, then use it. If your heart is prompted to give generously when needs arise, and you can do it with an overwhelming sense of joy, then you can know you have that gift. Certainly all of us should be giving to the Lord's work and meeting needs, but some people are uniquely gifted by God to give sacrificially and abundantly.

6. Leading (v. 8*c*)

a) Explained

The gift of leading ("ruling," Rom. 12:8) is the same as the gift of governments mentioned in 1 Corinthians 12:28. It means "to lead," "to manage," "to be in charge," or "to oversee." It is the gift of leadership, which involves the multiple skills of organizing, administrating, and motivating people to accomplish a task. The parallel gift of governments mentioned in 1 Corinthians is a translation of the Greek word *kubernētes*, which refers to the skill of piloting a ship.

The gift of ruling or governing belongs primarily to the elders and deacons of a church, who are required to manage their own households well (1 Tim. 3:4, 12). In fact, the only basic difference between a deacon and an elder is that an elder is able to teach. Deacons are not the primary articulators of the faith, but they are to be equally qualified in many of the other areas, including leadership ability. Paul qualifies the gift of leadership by saying it should be carried out with haste or zeal. That qualification expresses the importance and urgency of the gift.

b) Exemplified

God has designed the church to have leaders. In Acts 6 the apostles requested that the church find other men to carry on the administrative task of providing for the widows so that they could spend their time in the Word and prayer. The church needs administrators who can keep the church on course, operating with fairness, wisdom, efficiency, and humility. That kind of management ability is indispensable to the church. So if you have a gift in that area, make sure you are using it.

In my first years at Grace Community Church I realized that since there were not enough hours in the day for me to accomplish all that needed to be done, God would have to raise up members of the congregation to carry out various ministries. And He did! I remember when a member by the name of Vern Lummus came to me back in 1969 and said, "I believe we ought to have a tape ministry." I encouraged him to go ahead and start it. He said, "Do you mean *me*? I'm just telling you we need it." I said, "Right, and I'm just telling you that you ought to do it since it's your idea. Make it happen if you believe that's what the Spirit of God has laid on your heart." And I thank God that Vern made it happen.

I also remember when one of our members told me that the church needed a bus. So I told him that since God had laid that on his heart, maybe he could find one. He took me seriously and actually went out and bought one! When we had no women's ministry and some women recognized the need for one, they were the ones who got it started.

c) Exhorted

Recognizing a need and effectively coordinating what must be done to meet that need is how the gift of ruling or leadership operates. Those of you who have that gift should get involved in leading. If you see a need and you know what action can be taken to meet it, find some other people who are like-minded, and see what God might do as you begin to move out in ministry.

7. Showing mercy (v. 8*d*)

a) Explained

Showing mercy is having pity and compassion toward people in misery—the poor, the downtrodden, the imprisoned, and others who are faced with hardships. You find people with this gift participating in jail ministries, hospital visitation, and rescue missions for the homeless. They have a passion in their hearts for destitute people.

b) Exemplified

Jesus is the supreme model for those with this gift. Certainly He showed mercy. Near the beginning of His ministry He said, "The Spirit of the Lord is upon me, because he hath anointed me to preach the gospel to the poor; he hath sent me to heal the brokenhearted, to preach deliverance to the captives, and recovering of sight to the blind, to set at liberty them that are bruised" (Luke 4:18). Part of Jesus' ministry was to the poor and needy.

c) Exhorted

Paul exhorts those with the gift of showing mercy to do it with an attitude of cheerfulness. If you're going to minister to people who are miserable, you had better not be miserable yourself while you're doing it. Go with an attitude of joy. Don't say, "Oh, I've got to go down and help those losers again. I'm going to grit my teeth and do it." Ministry to people in need is to be done with an attitude of cheerfulness. In Proverbs 14 Solomon writes, "He that hath mercy on the poor, happy is he" (v. 21).

Conclusion

Paul doesn't give us a detailed technical definition of every gift and include all their parameters. He's providing a general list for believers to consider as they look to how they should respond to the mercies of God. His list covers the basic needs of the church: prophecy is proclamation, serving is operation, teaching is systematization, exhortation is motivation, giving is implementation, leading is mobilization, and showing mercy is commiseration. Although I proclaim and teach God's Word, others at Grace Church also proclaim and teach, as well as exhort, lead, serve, and care for fellow believers. That's the way the church is supposed to work.

John Owen, a Puritan writer of the seventeenth century, wrote *The Holy Spirit: His Gifts and Power* (Grand Rapids: Kregel, n.d.). He defined spiritual gifts as those elements without which the church could not subsist in the world, nor believers be useful to one another and the rest of mankind. He saw them as powers of the world to come, outworkings of the power of Christ for the establishment and preservation of His kingdom.

You shouldn't spend too much time trying to analyze your gift. Rather focus on Christ. As you strive to let the Spirit of God work in you, He will lead you to serve, which is when you will see your gift in action. Second Corinthians 3:18 says that as we gaze on the glory of the Lord we're progressively changed into His image by the Holy Spirit.

The Corinthians focused on the gifts rather than on the Lord who gave them. They were preoccupied with acquiring the prominent showy gifts, like selfish children who want to play with the biggest and best toy. Early twentieth-century hymn writer A. B. Simpson wrote these words:

> Once it was the blessing, now it is the Lord.
> Once it was the feeling, now it is His Word.
> Once His gifts I wanted, now the Giver alone.
> Once I sought healing, now Himself alone.

In seeking the Lord and walking with Him, we will find the gifts He has given us operating for His glory. The ministry of our gifts begins by recognizing the mercies of God and then offering Him our lives on a daily basis. We're to then humbly evaluate what our gifts are and begin to use them by ministering to the Body of Christ. If you haven't been doing that, then you need to consider Paul's exhortation to Timothy in 2 Timothy 1:6 to "stir up the gift of God, which is in thee."

Focusing on the Facts

1. Describe the gift of exhorting. Compare its relationship to the truth with the gifts of prophesying, serving, and teaching (see p. 61).
2. What are some of the different ways the gift of exhorting can be expressed (1 Thess. 5:14; see p. 61)?
3. What does it mean to give with liberality? How does that compare with the way the Pharisees gave (see p. 62)?
4. How did many of the believers in the early church at Jerusalem meet the needs of others (Acts 2:44-45; 4:34-37)? Why was it necessary to do that (see pp. 62-63)?
5. Define the gift of leading. Identify its parallel gift in 1 Corinthians 12:28 (see p. 63).
6. To whom does the gift of ruling primarily belong (see p. 63)?
7. Describe the gift of showing mercy. In what type of ministries might people with that gift be involved (see p. 65)?
8. Rather than spending a great deal of time trying to analyze your spiritual gift, on what should you focus? On what had the Corinthians wrongly focused (see p. 66)?
9. Summarize the process of how to use your gifts in the service of the Lord (see p. 67).

Pondering the Principles

1. You may not yet know in what area God has predominantly gifted you. However, as a Christian you have the responsibility to minister at least to a small degree in the seven areas of giftedness Paul mentions. Although you may not have the gifts of prophecy, teaching, or exhortation, you need to be proclaiming the truth to your neighbors, friends, relatives, and coworkers,

encouraging them to know God personally and grow spiritually (Matt. 28:18-20; 1 Thess. 5:14; 1 Pet. 3:15). You may not have the gifts of serving, giving, or showing mercy, yet you are called to express love for others in tangible ways (Rom. 12:13; Gal. 6:6-10; Phil. 4:15-18; 1 John 3:16-18). Look up the verses listed, and prayerfully think of some ways you could be ministering to others this week.

2. You may believe you need the gift of leading or administration before you can implement a ministry. But if you recognize a problem or a need that's not being met in your church, and God has placed a solution in your heart, be prayerfully determining how to implement your idea, and speak with your pastor. Unfortunately, people often recognize a need and assume that someone else will see it and meet it. Take the initiative to be a problem-solver in your church. Be sensitive to the needs around you and willing to help meet them.

Scripture Index

Topical Index

Moody Press, a ministry of Moody Bible Institute, is designed for education, evangelization, and edification. If we may assist you in knowing more about Christ and the Christian life, please write us without obligation: Moody Press, c/o MLM, Chicago, Illinois 60610.